The
CRIGGION BRANCH
of the Shropshire & Montgomeryshire
Light Railway

Roger Carpenter

WILD SWAN PUBLICATIONS LTD.

No. 8236 at Shrewsbury (Abbey) station with an excursion bound for Llanymynech on Bank Holiday Monday, 5th August 1935.

H. F. WHEELLER

AN OUTLINE HISTORY

DURING the autumn of 1860, a prospectus was published launching the 'West Midland, Shrewsbury and Coast of Wales Railway'. A truly optimistic venture from the railway mania period, its objective was to create an alternative route to Ireland. The proposed 90-mile route was intended to run from Shrewsbury to Portmadoc via Kinnerley, Porthywaen, the Tanat Valley, Llangynog, Llandrillo (by means of a tunnel over 1½ miles long, under the Berwyns) and Bala. An extension was also proposed to Porthdinllyn, on the Caernarvon coast near Nevin, at which point it was envisaged that a port would be built as an alternative to Holyhead, with a connecting service to Ireland. Like so many railway schemes mooted at this time, it generated little interest. The extensive engineering works of this proposal would have been very costly, and the 1861 Parliamentary session rejected the bill in the standard orders procedure; nothing further was heard of the scheme.

The following year saw the authorisation of the 'West Shropshire Mineral Railway', a line from Llanymynech to Westbury (Salop), on the then recently approved Shrewsbury and Welshpool Railway. The scheme was spearheaded by a Richard Samuel France, the proprietor of the limestone quarries on Llanymynech Hill. In 1863-4, an application to modify these powers was made, with a view to opening up the mineral resources of the Breidden Hills to rail transport, and providing a more convenient route; the junction with the Shrewsbury & Welshpool Railway was now to be at Red Hill, 2½ miles west of Shrewsbury, with running powers to the General station. It was also proposed to change the company's title to the 'Shrewsbury & North Wales Railway', to carry passenger traffic, and to construct two additional lines. The latter submission involved an extension from Llanymynech to Llanyblodwell, to gain access to the Nantmawr lime quarries, and a branch from Kinnerley to Criggion, to tap the granite quarries. Parliamentary consent was granted to all the proposals, with the exception of the running powers over the GWR & LNWR Joint line into Shrewsbury General station. Curiously,

earthworks exist at Red Hill, indicating that a temporary connection may have been made, or work on the junction had commenced prior to Parliament's refusal. Access to Shrewsbury was therefore gained by an independent line, running parallel to the Welshpool to Shrewsbury Railway eastwards from Red Hill,

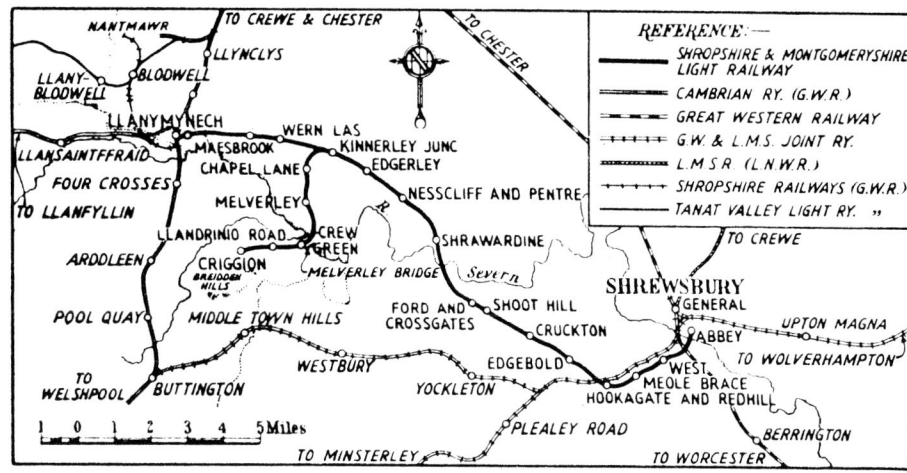

Map showing the Shropshire & Montgomeryshire Railway

crossing over the GWR & LNWR Joint Hereford line and the GWR Severn Valley line, turning northwards and dropping down to a terminus at Abbey Foregate, abutting the London Road.

Construction of the 28-mile route commenced at the quarries at Llanymynech, and progressed steadily along the whole of the authorised route. The contractor was R. S. France & Co., the work being carried out under the personal supervision of Mr. W. H. France.

Additional schemes to develop or expand the company were constantly under consideration, and one such plan involved a proposal to amalgamate with the Shrewsbury and Potteries Junction Railway. This company was promoted about the same time as the S & NWR, and proposed to connect Shrewsbury with Stoke-on-Trent by means of a line running via Market Drayton. Authorised in 1865 to link the Wellington to Market Drayton and Shrewsbury to Crewe lines, they decided to modify their plans, and join with the S & NWR. Formed in 1866, the combined undertaking became the 'Potteries, Shrewsbury and North Wales Railway', and sought Parliamentary approval for the Shrewsbury to Crewe

scheme. It also applied to revive the first stage of the former West Midland, Shrewsbury and Coast of Wales Railway scheme for an extension from Llanyblodwell to Llanygynog and Portmadoc. On this occasion, a lot of enthusiastic public interest was generated along the proposed course of the line, and, despite much strenuous opposition from the GWR and LNWR companies, Parliamentary approval was duly obtained. With hindsight, the company could have saved itself a lot of trouble and expense had the original scheme been followed through to a successful conclusion.

Under the powers conferred in 1865, the PS & NWR completed part of its proposed North Wales section, and the Board of Trade inspector passed the line. The Shrewsbury to Llanymynech line was duly opened for passenger traffic on Monday, 13th August 1866, as was the Criggion (or Breidden as it was then known) branch for goods services; the extension from Llanyblodwell to Nantmawr was also opened on the same day. The openings were notable for the lack of any ceremony, just a brief mention in the local newspaper, and some printed notices.

As in many other cases, the enthusiasm to open this rural line overshadowed any realistic account of the available traffic, and the PS & NWR soon found itself in trouble; indeed, the Bailiffs took possession of the line in December of that year, and the system ceased operations. Subsequently, a sale by private treaty was organised in order to dispose of various items of rolling stock and other effects. The sale was to be held at various stations on the 'main line', and this was announced in the press on 21st December 1866, on which day the line was formally closed. It took over two years to sort out the 'Potteries' line finances, and any thoughts that had been given to the construction of the Market Drayton line, or to the completion of construction work that had commenced at several other locations, were finally abandoned.

However, an attempt was made to reinstate working on the PS & NWR a couple of years later, and, during December 1868, main line services were re-introduced on a much reduced scale, followed on 2nd June 1871 by the re-opening of the Criggion branch. The Llanyblodwell extension was also re-opened in 1872. This revival, which involved both goods and passenger traffic, did not last long, and by 1880 the 'Potteries' Railway had again become a run-down concern. The sparsely-populated area through which the line ran, delightful though the scenery was, could not support it; even day trippers, who travelled over the line from Shrewsbury during the summer months, together with anglers during the fishing season, did not contribute sufficient to help the concern pay its way. The only revenue earning traffic of any magnitude was the granite, and even this decreased during the 1870s, giving rise to serious concern; this resulted in drastic economies in staff, with reduced maintenance of rolling stock and permanent way.

Yet, just as the expected axe was about to fall, another railway scheme which could have saved the line was being hatched by the Great Northern Railway, who underwent an enthusiastic expansion campaign during the 1870s. Having pushed their metals westwards through Derbyshire to Stafford in 1879, the GNR sought to gain access to the Cambrian Coast with the potentially viable East Midlands traffic. Their proposal involved running powers over the LNWR line from Stafford to Shrewsbury, thence via the 'Potteries' line to Llanymynech, and finally over the Cambrian main line to the coast. Alas, nothing ever came of the project, and the GNR came no further west than Stafford.

Meanwhile, the condition of the 'Potteries' line had deteriorated so badly that the Board of Trade demanded its closure on public safety grounds, and this took effect on 22nd June 1880. After this date, the Official Receiver appointed a small P.W. gang to carry out only the basic legal maintenance requirements, for which they used one small hand trolley.

For the next eight years, the line rested in a state of limbo, with vegetation gradually covering the track, timber-built bridges collapsing, whilst the wooden buildings soon became very dilapidated. The many items of rolling stock which had been left outside also rapidly showed signs of decay. However, the locomotives, which had been stored under cover, faired reasonably well, as did the permanent way (despite the undergrowth).

In March 1888, plans for restoration were submitted to Parliament under the auspices of the 'Shropshire Railways Bill', which proposed a new line from Shrewsbury to Hodnet, with onward running powers to Stoke via Market Drayton, over the Great Western and North Staffordshire Railways. A great deal of local support was generated, especially from tradesmen adjacent to the existing line who had suffered by the 1880 BoT closure. The Bill was incorporated in an Act of 7th August 1888, which resulted in the PS & NWR Company's liquidators, seeing the fate of their line looming in the distance, arranging for a public auction of all movable assets on 24th August 1888 at Abbey Foregate, Shrewsbury, where most of the rolling stock was at the time of the closure. The auction then moved along the line to the various station sites, where vehicles had been left in goods yard sidings.

After the stock sale, the way was clear for the new company to forge ahead with its plans to develop the old line, having obtained their order on 12th July 1889 (amended during the following month). After some wranglings with the shareholders and creditors of the PS & NWR, the new company took possession of the old 'Potteries' line on 19th September 1890 and arranged for a contractor, Messrs. Charles Chambers of Westminster, to rehabilitate the line within a twelve-month period. This involved the relaying of the main line to Llanymynech, the re-opening of the Abbey Foregate connection, the raising of Shrewsbury (Abbey Foregate) station above flood level, and the construction of a new approach line to replace the existing sharp descent. At this stage, the new company did not propose the immediate re-opening of the Breidden (or Criggion) branch, considering the extension to Market Drayton as more important. The next twelve months saw most of the main line re-sleepered and re-fenced, and the replacement of many bridges (which had previously been of timber construction) with brick, concrete or wrought iron structures; a start had also been made on raising the station at Shrewsbury. In July 1891, the severe financial difficulties being experienced by the company

The abandoned PS & NWR signal box at Kinnerley, in November 1902.

S. E. FOXDAVIES, CTY. C. C. GREEN

resulted in the contractor withdrawing his men; this action was followed by numerous legal suits, and the company was finally wound up, due to lack of funds.

Once again, the line assumed the role of a forgotten railway, with nature taking its course. When work had finished in July 1891, over half of the contracted work had been completed; most of the trackwork had been renewed, as had a few of the bridges, all of which effort was wasted, for it was to be another twenty years before the next moves towards re-opening were to be made. During 1902-4, the well-known railway historian, Mr. T. R. Perkins, traversed the whole system on foot, recording his findings in an excellent three-part article published in *The Railway Magazine* of May 1903, June 1903 and October 1904.

During the early years of this century, resolutions were passed by various local councils pressing for the line's re-opening, despite its already chequered career. These demands finally caught the attention of Colonel H. F. Stephens, who was a very enthusiastic supporter of the concept of light railways, and who considered that the line was worthy of development within the sphere of the recently introduced Light Railways Act. Once again, local support for a revival was very encouraging, and an application was sought during May 1907. After further legal negotiations had taken place, a Light Railway Order was issued by the Board of Trade on 11th February 1909, and the Shropshire & Montgomeryshire Light Railway came into being. In March 1909, a private meeting of potential supporters took place, with the Earl of Powis presiding; this resulted in the formation of a small committee, which was to visit the East Kent and the Kent & East Sussex Railways, both of which were under construction at the time. Their findings did much to aid local support for the new light railway, but it was not until the summer of 1910 that reconstruction work commenced, starting at Llanymynech (where the only physical connection to the national railway network existed).

Once the undergrowth had been cleared – and this had become very dense in places – a start was made with track relaying. Upon inspection, the 24ft rails and their chairs, which were the originals dating back to 1865, were found to be in

Llanymynech Junction, looking north, on 6th October 1931. The S & MR platforms are to the right. R. K. COPE

good condition, although those sleepers on the main line that had been laid un-creosoted during the 1888 renewals, were, in places, rotten; the PS & NWR sleepers on the Criggion branch were in much better condition. Apart from various modifications to some of the station layouts, the only new track laid was a connection to the GWR & LNWR Joint Shrewsbury–Welshpool line near Meol Brace, 1¼ miles from Shrewsbury. The only significant engineering work required was the rebuilding of Melverley Viaduct (on the Criggion branch), the previous PS & NWR timber structure having collapsed prior to 1902.

The stations were next to receive attention; the brick buildings were simply cleaned up, with doors and windows being replaced as necesssary, whilst the timber structures were either similarly refurbished or completely replaced by new timber constructions. A number of new halts and stations were also provided, although they were not all completed in time for the 1911 re-opening.

The original locomotive shed and workshops were situated at the Shrewsbury terminus, whilst a small locomotive shed was provided at Llanymynech. All of these facilities were demolished by the Shropshire Railways Company, and part of the Shrewsbury site was used by the Midland Wagon Company as part of its works. The S & MLR decided upon a central locomotive shed and workshops complex, and selected a site near the 'V' between the main line and the Criggion branch at Kinnerley.

The re-opening took place on Thursday, 13th August 1911, and after a ceremony conducted by the Mayor of Shrewsbury, some 200 invited guests joined the inaugural train with the Managing Director, Colonel H. F. Stephens. The train consisted of four bogie coaches, two 4-wheeled brake vans and (for the outward journey only) two Cambrian Railways saloons, hauled by an ex-LSWR 0–6–0 painted in olive green, and named *Hesperus*. The Criggion branch, which had remained closed due to unfinished work on Melverley viaduct, re-opened for parcels, goods and mineral traffic on Wednesday, 21st February 1912, and for passenger traffic the following August. In anticipation of greater output, due to the branch's re-opening, the Criggion Granite Quarry owners invested in new fixed equipment, including the erection of a new crushing plant.

The initial timetables showed three trains from Shrewsbury to Llanymynech and four in the reverse direction, with an additional return journey being operated on Thursdays and Saturdays. The Criggion branch service consisted of three return journeys, with an additional service on Wednesday and Saturday mornings. Both the main line and the branch had a Sunday service, which consisted of two return journeys on the former and one return journey on the latter; these must have been viable, because the railway made a net profit of £463 during 1912. This pattern of services did not change a great deal through to the late 1920s,

Shropshire and Montgomeryshire Railway.

TIME TABLE.

February, 1920, and until further notice.

	WEEK DAYS.											SUNDAY		
UP TRAINS.	a.m.	a.m.	a.m.	a.m.	a.m.	p.m.	p.m.	p.m.	p.m.	p.m.	p.m.	p.m.	p.m.	p.m.
Llanfyllin .... dep.			7 20		10 20		2 § 5		2 § 5		5 50			
Welshpool .... ,,			7 25		10 45		3 18		4 32		5 45			
Oswestry.............. ,,			8 15		10 50		3 45		3 45		7 50			
Llanymynech Jn. S&MR ,,			8 35		11 25	1 45	4 5		5 10		8 10			
Wern Las .... ,,			s		s	s	s		s			Service		
Maesbrook .... ,,			8 40		11 32		4 10		s		8 15	Suspended		
Criggion .... ,,			8 10			1 5		4 45	5 B 5					
Llandrinio Road ... ,,			8 15			1 8			s					
Crew Green for Alberbury, Coedway ,,			8 20			1 13		4 55	5 12					
Melverley .... ,,			8 27			1 18		5 5	5 16					
Kinnerley Junction ... ,,			8 47		11 45	2 0	4 20	5 10	5 30		8 25			
Nesscliff & Pentre...... ,,			8 55		11 52	2 6	STOPS		5 37					
Shrawardine.............. ,,			9 0		12 0	2 12			s					
Ford & Crossgates ..... ,,			9 13		12 15	2 35			5 55					
Cruckton.................... ,,			9 16		s	s			s					
Hanwood Road.......... ,,			9 19		12 25	2 45			6 5					
Redhill.................... ,,			9 24		12 35	s			6 10					
Meole Brace .... ,,			9 28		12 40	2 55			6 15					
Shrewsbury West...... ,,			s		s	s			s					
Shrewsbury S.& M.R. arr.			9 35		12 50	3 5			6 30					

	WEEK DAYS.											SUNDAY		
DOWN TRAINS.	a.m.	a.m.	a.m.	a.m.	a.m.	p.m.	p.m.	p.m.	p.m.	p.m.	p.m.	p.m.	p.m.	p.m.
Shrewsbury, S.& M.R. dep.					9 45		2 F 0	3 G 0		3c50	6 45			
Shrewsbury West........ ,,					s		s	s		s	s			
Meole Brace .... ,,					9 55		2 10	3 15		3 55	6 50			
Redhill.................... ,,					s		2 13	3 20		4 0	s			
Hanwood Road .... ,,					s		2 18	3 25		4 4	s			
Cruckton................ ,,					s		2 45	3 40		s				
Ford & Crossgates..... ,,					10 20		2 45	3 40		4 10	7 7			
Shrawardine........... ,,					s		2 55	3 50		4 20	s			
Nesscliff & Pentre ..... ,,					10 35		3 5	3 55		4 30	7 25			
Kinnerley Junction ... ,,		7 0	7 35	10 45	12 15	3 15	4 20	3 45	4 40	7 32				
Melverley............... ,,		7 7			D		4 25	3 52	4 47					
Crew Green for Alberbury, Coedway ,,		7 12			D		s	4 0	4 52					
Llandrinio Road ..... ,,		7 20			D			4 5	4 57					
Criggion............... ,,		7 25			12 50		4 45	4 15	5 0					
Maesbrook............. ,,			7 40	10 50		3 20	4 25			s				
Wern Las............. ,,			s	s		s	s							
Llanymynech Jn. S&MR arr.			7 50	11 0		3 30	4 35			7 45				
Oswestry.............. ,,			8 16	11 25		3 49	5 16			9 16				
Welshpool :...... ,,			8 56	11 22		6 8	6 8			8 35				
Llanfyllin ... . ,,			9 10	11 55		4 25	6 18			8 †40				

D—Stops to set down only.
F—Wednesdays Excepted.
G—Wednesdays Only.
S—Stops by Signal to pick up and set down on notice being given at Station or to Guard on joining Train.
§—On Saturdays leaves at 1·40 p.m.
†—Mondays and Saturdays only.
B—Wednesdays and Saturdays only.
Every effort will be made to connect with the Trains of other Companies as shown, but the same will not be guaranteed.

H. F. STEPHENS,
MANAGING DIRECTOR.

February, 1920. ABBEY STATION, SHREWSBURY.

The S & MR terminus at Shrewsbury, photographed on 9th October 1931. R. K. COPE

by which time the threat of the road motor was making itself apparent. The halts and stations were situated some distance from the places they purported to serve, which was a great disadvantage to the railway, especially in a district which was in any case sparsely populated.

Despite this handicap, the S & MR managed to maintain a passenger service, albeit with all the trains running mixed, which, because they were shunted at each station, did little to encourage potential passenger traffic. To encourage more passengers to use his lines and to reduce operating costs, Colonel Stephens introduced his famous back-to-back railcar sets, two of which were introduced onto the S & MR. Although they were cheap to operate, their noisy, vibratory and slow progress along the line made them unpopular with passengers and staff alike, and resulted in their early withdrawal. If anything, they accelerated the demise of the passenger services.

The Criggion branch service was the first to suffer rationalisation when, in September 1928, the daily (except Sunday) service of two return trips was reduced to Thursdays and Saturdays only; the service was foreshortened in October

1932, when the poor condition of the viaduct resulted in passenger trains being cut back to Melverley. In the meantime, the main line was suffering similar economies and, in the autumn of 1932, the last advertised timetable appeared. This showed a morning trip running from Kinnerley to Llanymynech, Shrewsbury, and back to Kinnerley, with a similar trip in the afternoon (the latter trip running at a later time on Mondays and Wednesdays). Additional trains were run on Saturdays, and these consisted of a midday working from Kinnerley to Llanymynech and back, together with two return journeys from Kinnerley to Melverley.

Almost without notice, the normal passenger service ceased as from 6th November 1933. However, the Bank Holiday excursions, which had been operating along the main line (with a connection to the branch) for a number of years, continued until 1937, when the daily goods train (which included a return trip up the Criggion branch) became the sole remaining working. This train was advertised in the LMS public timetable, and was the only way one could travel over the line in the late 1930s apart from

hiring *Gazelle* and her 4-wheel coach. Probably the most well-known instance of *Gazelle* being hired was on Sunday, 23rd April 1939, when she conveyed members of the Birmingham Locomotive Club, the trip proving so popular that it was repeated a week later to accommodate the overflow!

However, the tranquility was soon dispelled by the outbreak of war later that year, at which time the line was requisitioned by the War Department. In the hands of the Military, the line seemed to lose some of its sleepy charm (with perhaps the exception of the Criggion branch, which was not used for Department purposes, and consequently retained its character to the end).

During January and February 1940, there was prolonged heavy snow and ice which, when it melted, caused the Severn and Vyrnwy rivers to flood at abnormally high levels; the resultant floating ice and other debris damaged a number of vertical pier members on the upstream side of Melverley Viaduct. The branch was closed for eighteen months, from February 1940 until the late summer of 1941, during which time the quarry output was sent by road to the GWR

Meole Brace exchange sidings and signal box (with the S & M line in the foreground), looking westwards on 8th October 1931. About two miles further down the line, the S & M climbed over the GWR line to Welshpool before striking off north-westwards to Kinnerley and Llanymynech.
AUTHOR'S COLLECTION

station at Four Crosses. During this period, the BQC wagons sat idle at the quarries. During 1947, the engineers from the GWR's Shrewsbury District Bridge Department did some preliminary work on the viaduct, and in the following year, a contractor, Messrs. A. E. Farr Ltd. of Reading, constructed a new viaduct (which still survives, albeit in use as a road bridge). This new bridge only served its intended purpose for a little over ten years, the branch being closed in December 1959. The main line lasted only a couple of months longer, finally closing in February 1960 when the War Department decided to shut the last of the ordnance depots which were served by the railway.

The Criggion branch, to all intents and purposes, was a separate, self-contained unit from the main line; because of its lesser status, the branch retained its light railway atmosphere to the end. The main line, once it had been taken over by the War Department in 1941, lost this character; it assumed the appearance of a typical military railway, both in its fixed and rolling assets. After the takeover, the former company's rolling stock gradually went to the scrap heap, although *Gazelle* managed to survive, and was subsequently preserved. Despite intense War Department activity on the main line, the Criggion branch carried on much as it had before the war, conveying stone from the quarry; because it was not requisitioned, the branch was, in effect, worked as an extension of the BQC quarry lines by that company's Sentinel 0—4—0.

During 1948-9, the viaduct was reconstructed under the supervision of British Railways (Western Region) civil engineers, the resultant bridge being rather more substantial than the previous structures. This view, taken on 14th April 1949, looks across the new structure towards Kinnerley, whilst, on the right, the old S & MR bridge is being removed. J. G. VINCENT

In 1937, Melverley viaduct started to develop structural faults which, during 1940/1, became very serious at the Criggion end; as a safety precaution, the pattern of branch movements were therefore changed. The quarry's Sentinel propelled the loaded granite wagons from Criggion and, on arrival at the viaduct, proceeded to push the wagons across to the waiting S & M locomotive on the other side; empties were similarly worked, being propelled from Kinnerley. From 1942, the Sentinel was permitted to cross the viaduct at walking pace, and as a result was able to work through to Kinnerley, a practice which was to continue until the closure of the branch in December 1959 (when the remaining output was transferred to road transport).

As the branch was not transferred to the War Department, it remained in private hands until Nationalisation in January 1948 when it, together with the main line (which was released from military control at the same time) became part of British Railways (Western Region). It was only due to the quarry's support that the branch lasted as long as it did; without that patronage, it would probably have closed in the 1930s. Reclamation of the fixed assets was effected during 1960, and, although much of the former trackbed has now blended back into the landscape, making the course of the line difficult to follow, the stations and Melverley viaduct still remain (the latter, as previously mentioned, in use as a public road bridge).

THE ROUTE DESCRIBED

Kinnerley station, 6th October 1931, looking westwards from the road bridge towards Llanymynech. The Criggion branch can be seen curving away to the left, occupied by 'Collier' 0–6–0 No. 8108, which is shunting the daily branch freight. A rake of four-wheelers of MR, LSWR and NSR origins can be seen in the bay platform. The rake of LMS 5-plank opens standing at the Down platform is destined for Criggion quarry, in connection with the contract for the supply of road stone for the East Lancashire road scheme. One of the S & MR 'back-to-back' railcars can be seen at the far end of the goods yard (to the right). One unit appears to be standing on blocks, minus its chassis. Also visible in the goods yard is an ex-LSWR four-wheel three-compartment Brake Third, and one of the S & MR cattle vans. The black corrugated iron building on the Up platform is the goods shed, whilst the company's workshops and engine shed can be seen in the distance to the left. R. K. COPE

By the 1930s, light railways had reached their twilight years, and so it was with the Shropshire and Montgomeryshire. It would be of interest, therefore, to take a brief look at the Criggion branch in those halcyon years, before it faded into oblivion.

The Criggion branch diverged from the S & MR's main line at the western end of Kinnerley station, and curved away in a southerly direction. A bay was provided from the outset at Kinnerley to accommodate the branch train, although during the S & MR era, this was more often used to store coaching stock. The S & MR's locomotive shed and workshops were sited alongside the branch to the south of the junction with the main line, and contained an assortment of locomotives and rolling stock in various stages of decay. The line then followed a straight course for a short distance through flat farm land

Continued on page 19

The west end of Kinnerley station, looking towards Llanymynech on Saturday, 2nd October 1937, showing the pillar tank at the end of the Down platform serving both main and bay lines. By this time, even the excursion traffic had finished, leaving the sleepy line in the hands of freight trains. R. K. COPE

The road overbridge at the eastern end of Kinnerley station, looking towards Shrewsbury on 2nd October 1937; the timber side walls of the structure were painted yellow. The BQC wagons on the Down main were loaded with a consignment of granite awaiting despatch. The raised portion of the Down platform was used for the loading and unloading of milk and live-stock traffic.   R. K. COPE

The red brick station building on the Down platform and, behind, the station master's timber-built bungalow, photographed on Tuesday, 6th October 1931.
R. K. COPE

Kinnerley, on Saturday, 18th May 1929. The Passenger Brake Van, positioned against the raised section of platform to assist in loading, was an ex-MR vehicle, whilst the five-compartment coach originated from the North Staffordshire Railway. R. K. COPE

The daily train from Shrewsbury alongside the Up platform at Kinnerley on Monday, 4th October 1937, behind 'Collier' 0–6–0 No. 8182. The private owner wagon is owned by John Potts & Co. Ltd. of Macclesfield, the scene itself being so typical of light railway operations in the inter-war years. R. K. COPE

A morning excursion train from Shrewsbury to Llanymynech pauses at Kinnerley station on Bank Holiday Monday, 5th August 1935. The Ford railcar set is standing at the adjacent platform, forming the connecting service to the Criggion branch.   H. F. WHEELLER

During the early afternoon of the same day, passengers await the arrival of another excursion train. The covered ground frame cabin on the left was supplied by Tyers of Shrewsbury in 1911, and contained 13 levers, one of which was spare.   H. F. WHEELLER

0−6−0 'Collier' No. 8108 approaching the empty stock in the bay line at Kinnerley, on Bank Holiday Monday, 5th August 1935.

H. F. WHEELLER

During the afternoon of 5th August 1935, 0−6−0 'Collier' No. 8236 stands at the Down platform with a Shrewsbury to Llanymynech excursion, whilst sister engine No. 8108 waits in the bay with the Criggion branch service.

H. F. WHEELLER

An ex-LMS (LNWR) 'Collier' 0–6–0 No. 8108 heading a summer afternoon excursion train out of the bay at Kinnerley on Bank Holiday Monday, 5th August 1935. The stock on this occasion consists of an ex-MR Passenger Brake and two ex-North Staffs four-wheelers.

H. F. WHEELER

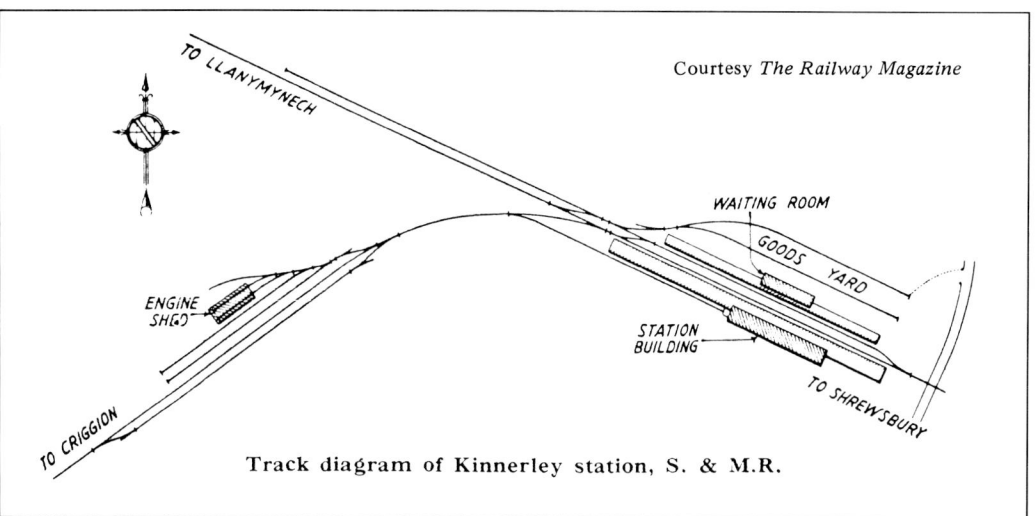

Courtesy *The Railway Magazine*

Track diagram of Kinnerley station, S. & M.R.

S & MR locomotive shed and works, Kinnerley Junction, on 5th August 1935. The left-hand line from the rearmost point led to the bay platform at Kinnerley. H. F. WHEELLER

The Up Home branch signals at Kinnerley Junction on 5th August 1935. These are of Tyer's pattern, the top arm indicating branch to Up main movements and the lower arm, branch to bay platform. The signals were situated at the northern entrance to the locomotive yard, about 100 yards short of the junction with the main line, on the Up side of the tracks. The timber building was probably used by the PW Department. H. F. WHEELLER

The S & MR engine shed and workshops, Kinnerley, on 1st September 1937, with the Criggion line passing between the coaches and the wagon. The gently decaying ex-MR bogie stock is standing on the loop line which ran alongside the branch at this point, whilst the open wagon in the foreground carried engine coal supplied by the Gresford Colliery, Wrexham. The vaned water pump could be seen for some considerable distance from the shed/workshop and was something of a local landmark.
R. K. COPE

A slightly closer view of the locomotive shed, in April 1935.   AUTHOR'S COLLECTION

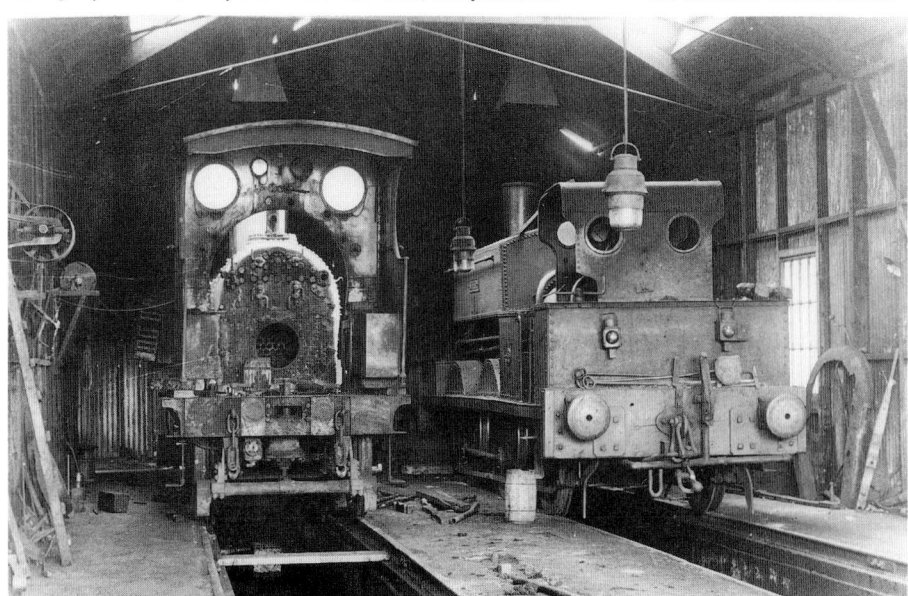

The water tower and the wind-operated water pump at Kinnerley shed, pictured in 1935. The cab of the ex-LSWR 0–6–0 'Ilfracombe Goods' No. 5 Pyramus *can be seen to the right of the tower, the engine itself having been cut up a couple of years previously.*
J. H. L. ADAMS

Inside Kinnerley locomotive shed c.1923 with one of the 'Ilfracombe Goods' 0–6–0s undergoing extensive repair. On the right is the Bury 0–4–2ST No. 2 Severn *(formerly* Hecate*).*
LENS OF SUTTON

Kinnerley engine shed, seen from the Criggion branch, probably in the 'thirties. AUTHOR'S COLLECTION

A tranquil scene outside the workshops at Kinnerley, on 5th August 1935. The view typifies the light railway scene, with parts, materials and discarded items scattered around. The smoke was rising from the steam-driven workshop machinery in the distance beyond the withdrawn 'Ilfracombe Goods' Thisbe. *Other surplus stock included two ex-GER coaches, the remains of 0−4−2ST No. 2* Severn, *a side tank from the 'Terrier'* Dido, *one of the S & MR cattle vans, and what could be the driving wheels from one of the scrapped 'Terriers'.* H. F. WHEELLER

The Criggion branch at Kinnerley, looking northwards towards the company's workshops, 4th October 1937. There were clearly no funds available for weedkilling by this time! R. K. COPE

One mile to the south of Kinner-ley was the small halt at Chapel Lane, pictured here on 20th July 1949. The PW hut was a wartime alteration, having previously served as a waiting shelter which originally stood at the far (northern) end of the platform ramp. Both the running line and the siding have been re-sleepered.
R. K. COPE

Chapel Lane Halt, photographed during 1933, looking down the branch towards Criggion from the ungated level crossing. The wagons on the right are empty BQC vehicles.   R. W. KIDNER

Chapel Lane Halt c.1933, with an unusual passenger occupying the platform ramp, having bypassed the cattle grids.

COLLECTION
LES DARBYSHIRE

before reaching Chapel Lane Halt, just over one mile from Kinnerley.

This halt was situated immediately to the south of the ungated Chapel Lane level crossing, the line on either side of which was protected by cattle guards. Chapel Lane Halt consisted of a short, stone-faced platform, edged with blue brick and backfilled with ash. Situated on the eastern side of the line, the platform was just long enough to accommodate one coach, and was provided with a timber waiting shed at the foot of its north-facing ramp. Goods facilities comprised one short siding, capable of holding six wagons, situated opposite the platform; the weed-covered rusty rails indicate that it seldom saw any use. Beyond the halt, the hedgerows and trees clustered alongside the line, features which, together with the alternating fields and copses, are typical of this part of Shropshire, and which form the total landscape throughout the branch's five-mile course. Having passed over another ungated crossing, a

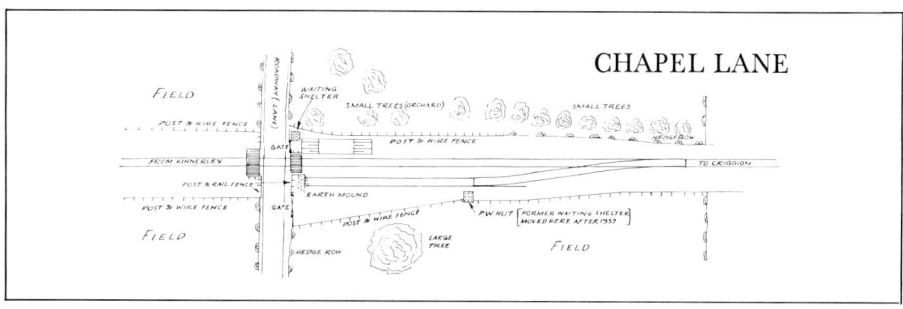

Looking north towards Kinnerley, this view was taken from the ungated level crossing of Chapel Lane Halt on 1st September 1937. The improvised telegraph poles made from tree trunks were a feature of the line.
R. K. COPE

The ungated occupation crossing between Chapel Lane Halt and Melverley, facing Kinnerley, on 20th July 1949.
R. K. COPE

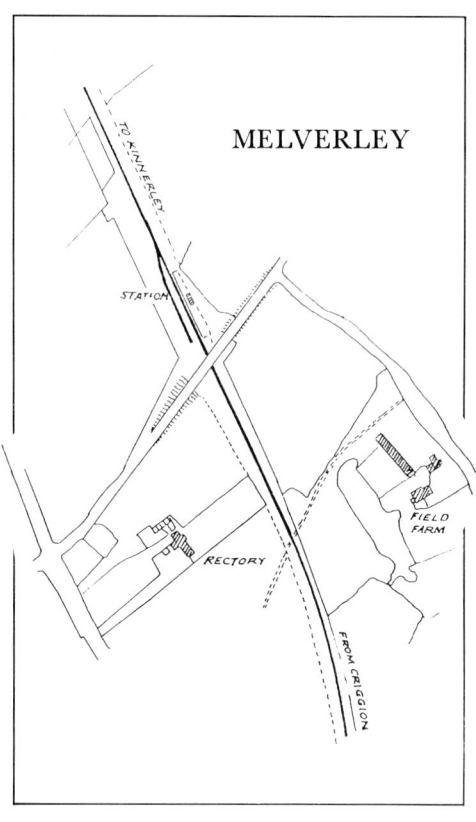

MELVERLEY

Melverley station's sylvan setting is well conveyed by this wartime view, taken during the summer of 1942.   S. H. P. HIGGINS

gentle, left-hand curve signals the approach to Melverley station, two miles from Kinnerley.

Located on the eastern side of the line, the red brick-faced platform (capable of holding two bogie coaches) was provided with a small red brick building, dating from the line's re-opening of 1871; this structure accommodated the station booking office and waiting room. Opposite the platform was a goods siding with a capacity of six wagons, often being occupied by empty granite wagons in addition to general goods vehicles. Beyond the station, the line was crossed by a lane (which connects the scattered hamlets of Melverley and Ponthen) by means of a curious seven-arched stone overbridge. This was one of the railway's more notable civil engineering features, being built to this design to allow flood water to escape, the River Severn being liable to flooding in this locality. To the south of the bridge, the line passed through a dense copse of undergrowth and trees

The station building at Melverley was constructed in red brick, with a grey slate roof. Judging by the variation in the end wall, it seems likely that a lean-to may have been situated there at some time, whilst alongside appears to be a bricked-up doorway. 6th October 1931.   R. K. COPE

The approach to the road bridge, on 20th July 1949. The bridge was demolished during the 1960s, soon after the track was lifted.   R. K. COPE

Melverley, seen from the road bridge on 6th October 1931, facing Kinnerley. Clearly, some re-sleepering of trackwork is about to take place, whilst the rails and chairs would invariably be re-used.
R. K. COPE

The tree-lined route of the railway to the south of the road bridge at Melverley, on 2nd October 1937. The vegetation on the right of the picture was cut back shortly after this view was taken, probably as a fire precaution, although it is doubtful whether the track received similar attention.

A final view of the seven-arch road bridge at the southern end of Melverley station. Substantially constructed in the local Breidden Hill grey stone, the bridge arches were lined with red brick. 2nd October 1937.
R. K. COPE

A short distance to the south of Melverley station, a side road serving the village crossed the line. This crossing was provided with gates when the line was opened in the 1860s, though after the re-opening in 1912 these were removed and cattle guards fitted as shown. This photograph illustrates the gatekeeper's house on 2nd October 1937. looking towards Criggion.
R. K. COPE

Just under a mile to the south of Melverley station, the line crossed the River Severn by means of the viaduct illustrated. This summer 1942 view of the viaduct shows the Breidden Quarry Company's Sentinel crossing cautiously with a train of empties for Criggion.
S. H. P. HIGGINS

Built in 1911, this structure replaced the earlier, rather flimsy timber bridge constructed by the PS & NWR; by that year, the original had long since collapsed, and most of it swept away. This c.1914 view of the S & MR viaduct clearly shows the wooden piles that gave so much trouble during the '30s and '40s. LOCAL STUDIES, SHREWSBURY

Melverley viaduct, looking across the spans towards Crew Green, on 5th August 1935. H. F. WHEELLER

Decking on the viaduct was sparse, as can be seen in this photograph, taken on 1st September 1937. On the far side, the line curved through 90 degrees to the left, heading north to Kinnerley.
R. K. COPE

Crew Green station was situated a short distance to the west of Melverley viaduct, just over 3 miles from Kinnerley; it also served the farming hamlets of Coedway and Alberbury. Set amidst typical Shropshire border landscape, the station consisted of a timber platform with a shelter at its eastern ramp, and a single siding with a grounded van body for the meagre goods traffic. This view from Crew Green station platform was taken on 1st September 1937, facing Kinnerley, showing the very overgrown track. The platform seat originated from the former Wolseley-Siddeley railcar set. Crew Green was the first of the stations along the line to be located in Wales, in which country the branch remained for the rest of its journey to the terminus.   R. K. COPE

The timber platform at Crew Green station was removed c.1940; this view, taken just before the outbreak of war, shows the platform in its final months of existence. The gate by the crossing at the Kinnerley end of the station gave access to the goods yard.   LENS OF SUTTON

This view, looking towards Criggion, shows the passenger facilities as seen from the level crossing, on 6th October 1931.
R. K. COPE

This photograph shows the goods facilities at Crew Green station, as seen from the westerly platform ramp, looking towards Criggion, on 1st September 1937. The grounded ex-MR 8-ton van body served as a goods shed and booking office, whilst the corrugated iron camping huts (refer to text) can be seen in the distance. Coal was sold by the wagonload by a Mr. Griffiths, who toured the area on a bicycle touting for trade.
R. K. COPE

before it re-entered the familiar scene of hedgerows and fields. After taking a gentle right-hand curve, it passed over yet another ungated level crossing, complete with a former PS & NWR red brick gate-keeper's cottage. The line then began a gentle curve to the west, before crossing the River Severn on the Melverley viaduct. Having passed over a further ungated level crossing, the line descended towards the river banks, before entering Crew Green station, 3¼ miles from Kinnerley.

Situated on the south side of the line, the platform was constructed in timber by the S & MR, and was just long enough for two bogie coaches; the original PS & NWR platform had disappeared long before the 1912 reconditioning. A timber waiting shed was provided at the foot of the platform, alongside the level crossing. To the west of the station, a six-wagon siding was located on the northern side of the line, with an ex-Midland Railway 8-ton van body mounted on brick piles to serve as a goods shed and booking office. At the time of the 1912 re-opening, it was hoped to be able to recommence working of the former Belan Bank quarry on a larger scale, and to exploit coal reserves at Crew Green and the surrounding district. For this purpose a syndicate

A closer view of the siding and goods shed and booking office, looking towards Kinnerley in April 1950.
G. F. BANNISTER

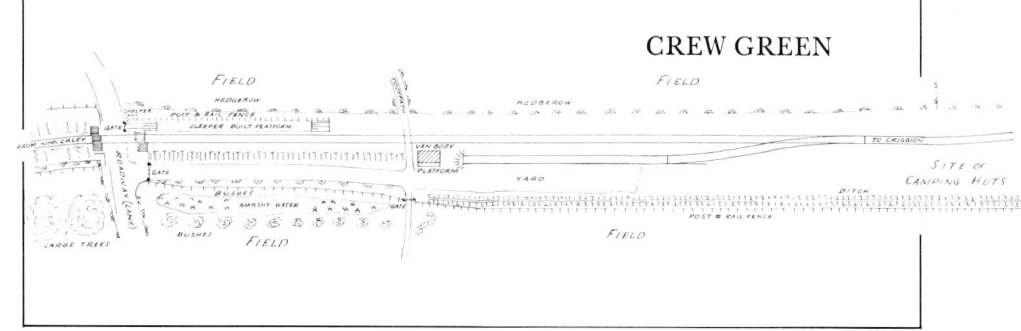

CREW GREEN

was formed, but the outcome of their deliberations is not known; there had been coal mines at Bausley in the 19th century belonging to the Leightons, and it is possible that an attempt was made to re-open them. During the 1920s, when the S & MR was struggling to maintain the passenger services on a viable footing, they even hired out boats and camping huts from the station, the river being in close proximity.

After the straight section through the station, the line then curved gently to the left, passing to the north of the old Belan Bank quarry. At one time, these workings had a short tramway, which crossed the branch by means of a wrought-iron bridge on its way down to the river. It is not known if the quarry was ever served by the railway during its workings in the 1860-80 period. The line then gently changed course to head in a south-westerly direction, before passing over another ungated occupation level crossing; a sharp left-hand curve then signified the

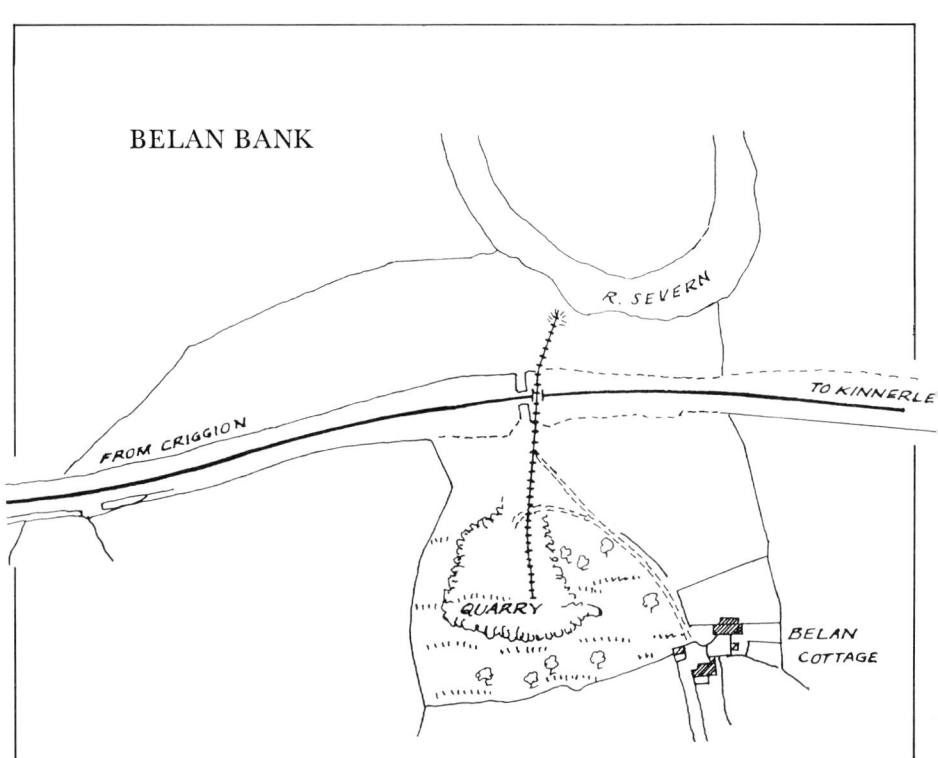

BELAN BANK

The Belan Bank Quarry line crossed the Criggion branch by means of a stone and iron bridge, seen here on 5th August 1935. The structure carried the narrow (around 2ft) gauge track of 'Jubilee'-style sections between the quarry and the river, where the small tub wagons used by the company were discharged into waiting barges. The quarry seems to have become disused by the late '30s. It is believed that the owner of the quarry had an 'agreement' with the S & M to tip stone chippings into wagons standing on the S & M line below the bridge, although this practice is understood to have been 'unofficial'! The quarry was sited on farmland, and the farmer was permitted to use the bridge to cross his livestock over the branch.

H. F. WHEELLER

The penultimate station on the line was Llandrinio Road, seen here in the middle distance. This view, which is dominated by the bulk of Breidden Hill, was taken looking east on 5th August 1935.

H. F. WHEELLER

proximity of Llandrinio Road station, some 4¼ miles from Kinnerley.

Before entering the station, the line passed another ungated level crossing of the road bearing the same name. Adjacent to the crossing was another of the old PS & NWR gate-keepers' cottages, to the same design as the one near Melverley (and at other principal S & MR level crossings), being constructed in red brick with a grey slate roof. Immediately beyond the crossing, on the south side of the line, was the red brick-faced platform; as at Melverley, this was just long enough for two bogie ·coaches. The platform was surmounted by an old van body (which at one time acted as a booking office, shelter and store), a seat and, at the Criggion end, a small cattle dock. Goods accommodation consisted of a short siding opposite the platform, with a capacity of six wagons. Behind the platform, the tree-clad peak of Breidden Hill loomed in the distance. Leaving Llandrinio Road, the line followed a relatively straight course

The ungated level crossing, Llandrinio Road, looking towards Kinnerley on 4th October 1937.
R. K. COPE

Situated one mile beyond Crew Green, Llandrinio Road station incorporated features common to the other small wayside S & MR stations that had been inherited from the PS & NWR, a short platform, level crossing with gatekeeper's house, and a single siding (situated in this instance behind the house). This view was taken on 6th October 1931, looking towards Criggion.
R. K. COPE

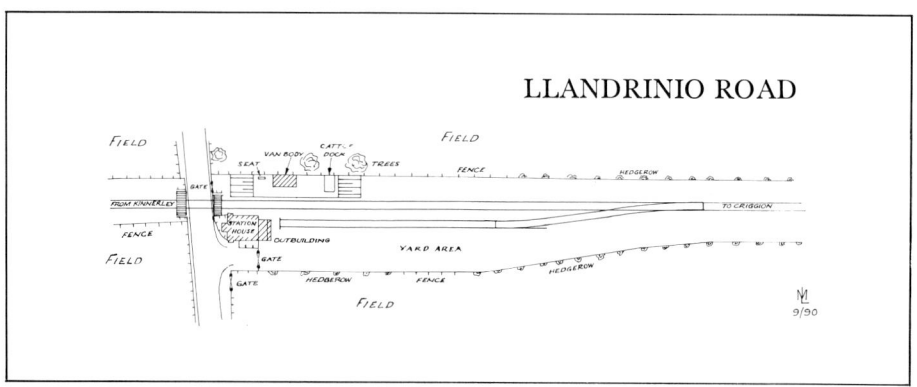

LLANDRINIO ROAD

Llandrinio Road, facing Kinnerley, in February 1948. Most of the siding accommodation on the line seems to have been used to store loaded or empty BQC wagons, and, in this case, vehicles containing wait-order crushed stone.
G. F. BANNISTER

A view of the platform at Llandrinio Road, looking towards Kinnerley, c.1937. The small, rather makeshift cattle pen was the only example on the branch, and had been removed by 1948. LENS OF SUTTON

through a landscape, becoming increasingly more dominated by Breidden Hill, as it approached the scattered community of Criggion.

Nearing the station (5¼ miles from Kinnerley), the line swung once more to the left, to be accompanied by a loop line on the inside of the curve until the platform was reached. Nestling at the foot of the Breidden Hill's tree-clad slopes, the platform was again on the south side of the line, but it was longer than all the others, with a capacity of three bogie coaches. Office accommodation consisted of a small red brick building, almost identical to that at Melverley. Opposite the platform was yet another red brick crossing keeper's cottage, to the same design as the others; originally, these houses provided accommodation for gate keepers at the more important crossings which, in the

The driver of the Ford railcar locking the catch point at the approach to Criggion station; the start of the loop line can be seen beyond. 5th August 1935.

H. F. WHEELLER

The terminus at Criggion, looking from the platform over the run-round loop towards Kinnerley on 18th May 1929. In this view the loop was housing the inevitable BQC wagons.
R. K. COPE

Looking westwards through Criggion station towards the quarry extension, on 14th October 1939. The track was relaid during 1938/39 with flat-bottomed rail, clearly seen in this photograph. The lean-to toilet facilities on the eastern end of the station building were probably similar to those which existed at one time on the Melverley building. Both cattle guard and gates were fitted to the level crossing beyond the gatekeeper's house.
J. E. VINCENT

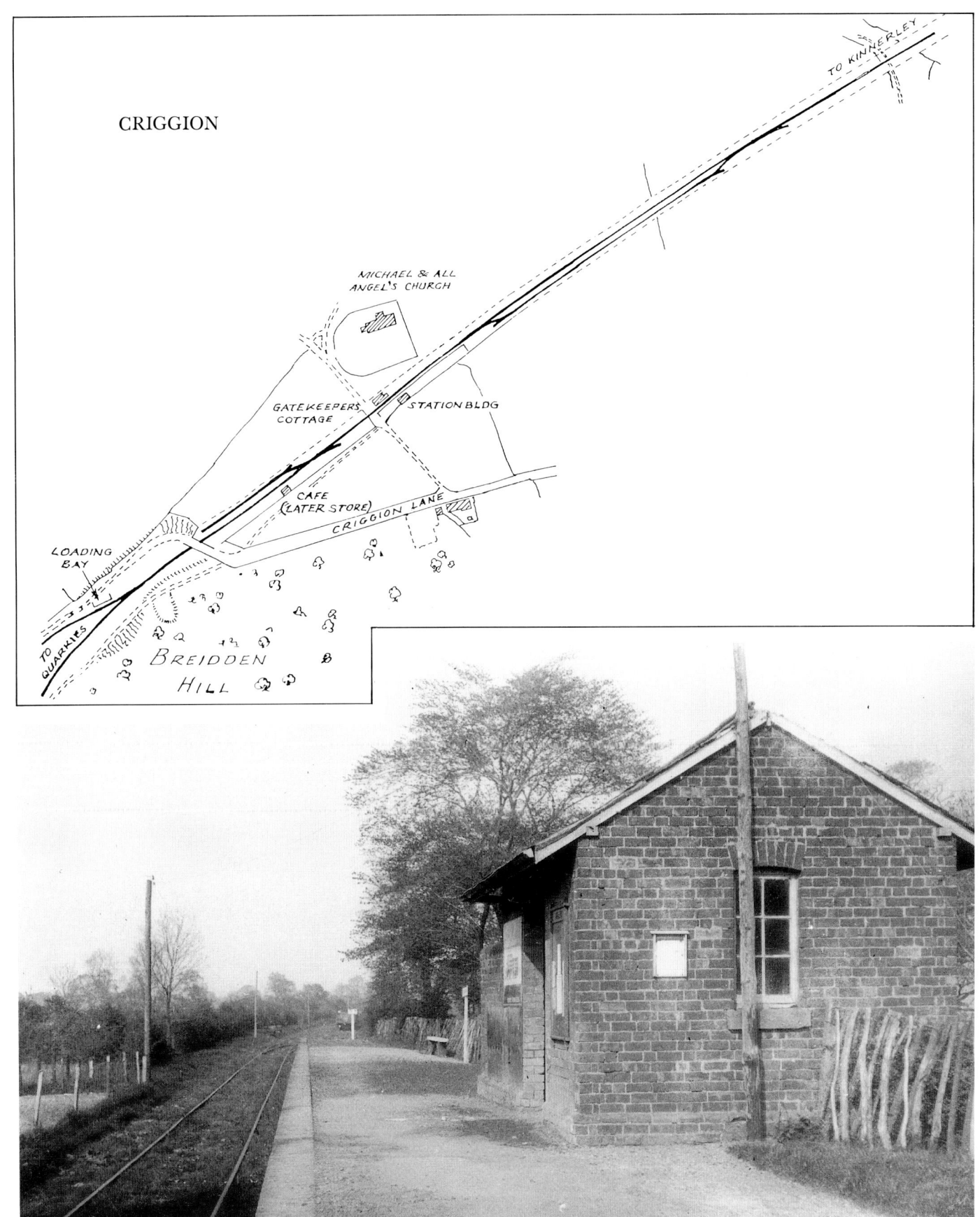

Criggion was situated some 5¼ miles from Kinnerley, and is pictured here on 18th May 1929, looking towards the junction station. Like Melverley, Criggion possessed a brick-built station building, albeit quite basic in design.
                                                                                                                                                                      R. K. COPE

The station area, as seen from Criggion Lane (which ran along the foot of Breidden Hill), looking north, on 7th October 1931.   R. K. COPE

Criggion station on 5th August 1935, with the Ford railcar set at the platform on a summer excursion working from Kinnerley. H. F. WHEELLER

Criggion station, against a back-drop of Breidden Hill, showing the two huts (centre of picture) which were in turn used for serving refreshments.

'Potteries' days, were fitted with gates, these being removed when the line was re-opened as a light railway in 1911-12.

Beyond the platform, the line crossed a road by one of the now familiar level crossings as a ¾-mile-long mineral extension to serve the Breidden Hill Quarries. Criggion goods yard was served by a siding branching off to the right immediately after the level crossing, having a capacity of six wagons (this was increased to fifteen wagons during the 1940s). On the opposite side of the running line was a storage shed; this was a circular corrugated iron design, which appears to be unique to the Colonel Stephens empire, having been purchased from the War Department during the 'twenties. The shed appears to have been in use as a cafe for a while at Criggion, whilst three others at Crew Green station were available for hire as camping huts! Beyond the goods siding was a single arch brick overbridge carrying Criggion Lane, a road which skirts the lower slopes of Breidden Hill, serving the scattered community of Criggion. The railway, now cutting into the hill's densely-wooded lower slopes, finally fanned out into several sidings which served both the quarry and its crushing plant, the ultimate terminus of the S & MR's Criggion branch.

A view of Criggion station in 1947, facing Kinnerley.   S. H. P. HIGGINS

Beyond the station's level crossing, the line continued for nearly a mile to the quarries, which were not only the sources of the branch's finance, but latterly that of the S & MR system too! This photograph, looking towards the workings from the level crossing on 5th August 1937, shows the remains of the circular corrugated iron structure which purportedly served as a storage shed, café, and even a boating hut (although the river was a good half-mile away). The bridge in the background carried Criggion Lane over the railway. H. F. WHEELLER

The eastern end of the BQC's workings, viewed from the Criggion Lane overbridge on 4th October 1937. The crushing plant was situated around the corner to the left. The interlaced sleepering on the point had been a common practice on some railways at one time. R. K. COPE

BREIDDEN QUARRY Co.

The Breidden Quarry Company (and its predecessor, the 'Granomac') was served by an extension of the branch line from Criggion station into the north-western slopes of the hill. Several sidings were provided at the site, more especially to afford accommodation for those wagons awaiting loading at the crushing plant.

Much of the quarry track was of flat-bottomed rails, spiked directly onto the sleepers, and was laid in a ballast of earth mixed with stone dust and waste.

A small engine shed was provided for the quarry locomotive, being located on the Criggion side of the stone crushing plant.

At one stage, a 2ft gauge tramway operated between the quarry face and the standard gauge sidings, and was known to be in use c.1914 until c.1930, when its

Another view of the loading bank, with the Sentinel arriving with a train of stone; the view looks east, towards the overbridge and Criggion station, April 1950.   G. F. BANNISTER

The quarry loading bank, on 4th October 1937, with the Criggion Lane overbridge in the background.   R. K. COPE

The end of the line at Breidden quarry, Criggion, with a party of enthusiasts reboarding the War Department inspection car which had conveyed them on the trip down the Criggion branch. 21st September 1958.
H. C. CASSERLEY

function was replaced by road transportation.

The quarry line was originally worked by *Jack*, a Bagnall 0−4−0ST built in 1901, and purchased by the quarry company from the ROD about 1919. This engine had originally been owned by the Cliffe Hill Granite Co. of Leicestershire, and after a useful spell at Criggion, was scrapped at the quarry c.1930.

Jack was replaced by the 0−4−0 Sentinel, built in 1927 (works No. 7026), and this latter engine worked until 1962 when it, too, was scrapped on site. The rail traffic via the branch had ceased in December 1959.

Breidden quarry on 2nd March 1941, showing the Sentinel and train standing outside the engine shed. J. G. VINCENT

LOCOMOTIVE AND TRAIN WORKING

A general view of Kinnerley shed in August 1926, showing Gazelle, *an ex-LBSCR 'Terrier' No. 8* Dido *(in steam), ex-LSWR 'Ilfracombe Goods' No. 6* Thisbe, *and another 'Terrier', No. 9* Daphne. *The two 'Terriers' were originally* Millwall *and* Earlswood *respectively, and were 'withdrawn' from service on the S & MR in 1932 along with a third example, No. 7* Hecate.
H. C. CASSERLEY

Details of the locomotives and passenger stock used on the line during the pre-Colonel Stephens era are sparse, but presumably one of the tank engines and a couple of the PS & NWR four-wheel coaches sufficed. Goods workings probably utilised the same engines, hauling wagons from the quarry company, the company itself, and perhaps visitors from other pre-Grouping railways.

However, much more is known of the Colonel Stephens era, when the company started off with six locomotives to handle the traffic. During its lifetime, the S & MR possessed, at one time or another, fourteen steam engines (excluding those engines which had been borrowed). Of these, six were 0-6-0 tender engines which, with a 'main line' of 20 miles, were more suitable than the tank engines. Also in use were two railcar sets, which were purchased in the late '20s in an attempt to run the passenger services more economically, a decision which had the reverse effect. The railcars, due to their unpopularity, lost a lot of passengers, and were soon withdrawn from service (public opinion on the West Sussex, and the Kent and East Sussex Railways was more

favourable, and they lasted much longer in public service on those lines).

Perhaps the line's most famous locomotive was No. 1 *Gazelle*, a tiny, toylike machine, now happily preserved. *Gazelle* was built in 1893 by the engineering firm of Alfred Dodman & Co. at their Highgate Works, King's Lynn, to the special order of a William Burkett, who was an influential East Anglian businessman with an eccentric love for railway locomotives. He carried a lot of influence within the organisations of the GER and the M & GNJR, and had the locomotive constructed to enable him to operate it for his own business trips over their metals.

Stabled at Lynn, the engine travelled widely, and was even noted at Chesterfield on one occasion. Constructed as a 2-2-2 well tank, with four passenger seats in the rear of the cab, it weighed 5 tons 6 cwt, and must have been one of the smallest standard gauge locomotives ever constructed. In 1910, it was put up for sale by T. W. Ward, and was purchased by Colonel Stephens for use as an inspection unit on the S & MR, who had it rebuilt as an 0-4-2 well tank at Bagnalls of Stafford shortly afterwards. Although she went to

Kinnerley in June 1911, she was back at Bagnalls later that year for further modifications including the covering-in of the cab and rear seating accommodation, together with the addition of a step. In this form she was returned from Bagnalls, and was put to work on the newly re-opened Criggion branch in 1912. Hauling an ex-LCC horse tramcar, she operated the branch service until it was reduced in 1928, when both were put out to grass at Kinnerley locomotive shed.

In 1936, Mr. W. H. Austin, who succeeded the Colonel as Engineer and General Manager for the whole of the late Colonel's light railway empire, decided to restore *Gazelle* for operation as an inspection unit on the line. After all the bits and pieces had been collected from the undergrowth (she had been partly dismantled during her years of storage), *Gazelle* disappeared into the workshops. She reappeared in June 1937, resplendent in olive green livery lined out in black and white, with red buffer beams, red connecting rods, brown frames, and wheels finished in olive green; the safety valve dome and nameplates were of polished brass. It was also the intention to provide

another small, lightweight four-wheel coach for her to haul, the former LCC tramcar's body being beyond repair; however, its chassis was serviceable, so it was put to good use carrying a body obtained from the Selsey Tramway's Wolseley-Siddeley railcar set. Like *Gazelle*, it was finished in olive green, and was utilised for inspection trips and the occasional private hire, the most famous being the Birmingham Locomotive Club's outings in April 1939.

When the War Department took control, *Gazelle* was actively used for PW work in the various military yards that sprang up alongside the main line, until she was withdrawn for the second time in 1945, and put into open store at Kinnerley. However, the WD took the locomotive to heart and in May 1950, when she became nominally BR (Western Region) property, a decision was made to preserve her. During the following month, *Gazelle* was transferred to the WD on permanent loan, being sent to the Royal Engineers (Railway Operating Division) camp at Longmoor, in Hampshire. In June 1950, she was fully repaired and repainted, before being mounted on a plinth outside the main depot buildings until its closure in 1970; after a short period in store, she was transferred to the Military Transport Museum at Beverley, Yorkshire, after an interim visit to the National Railway Museum at York.

In *Gazelle's* absence, the branch passenger workings were usually in the hands of an 0-4-2 saddle tank *Hecate*, which was No. 2 in the S & MR's lists. This locomotive was purchased from the Griff Colliery Company, and was re-conditioned and fitted with vacuum brake equipment by Bagnalls of Stafford before being delivered to the railway. She was constructed in the 1840s by Bury, Curtis & Kennedy of Liverpool for the Shrewsbury and Hereford Railway as an 0-6-0 tender engine, and passed into the ownership of the LNWR before being purchased by the Griff Colliery Company, who rebuilt her as an 0-4-2ST. The S & MR initially named her *Hecate*, but this was shortlived, for she was renamed *Severn* in 1916. At the time of purchase, she was put to work on the Criggion branch, working mixed trains in company with *Gazelle* and her tramcar. During the early '20s, she was relegated to granite train duties, which she worked until being put out to grass at Kinnerley in 1929

Gazelle with the ex-LCC tramcar at Kinnerley shed, c.1928. This view clearly shows the alterations carried out by Bagnall to Col. Stephens' specifications in 1911.
R. C. RILEY

The lineage of No. 2 Severn *went back as far as 1840, when she was constructed as an 0-6-0 tender engine by Bury, Curtis & Kennedy. She was purchased as an 0-4-2ST by the S & MR around the time of the Great War, being named* Hecate *until 1916. She was withdrawn in 1931.*
AUTHOR'S COLLECTION

S & MR No. 4 Morous, *pictured in the early days. This engine was a Manning Wardle 0-6-0T, built in 1866. It was used on the line for some time during the early period and transferred down to the Selsey Tramway, probably in the late 'twenties, remaining there until the closure of that line in 1935.*
AUTHOR'S COLLECTION

(although she was not officially withdrawn until 1931). She was finally cut up in April 1937, after many of her parts had been used to keep the other S & MR locomotives going.

The branch was also operated by one of the S & M's 'Terrier' 0−6−0Ts during the late 'twenties.

Of the other locomotives in the stud that were associated with the Criggion branch, the most well-known were the three ex-LSWR 'Ilfracombe Goods' 0−6−0s: No. 3 *Hesperus*, which was built in 1874 by Beyer Peacock to Mr. Beattie's design, being purchased in January 1911 for the opening of the line; No. 5 *Pyramus*, built in 1874, was purchased in the following November, and No. 6 *Thisbe*, built in 1873, was purchased in May 1916. Upon arrival, they were fitted with vacuum brake for passenger working, and repainted in the S & MR livery. Nos. 5 and 6 were finished in blue, lined out in red, with brass nameplates and oval-shaped cabside numberplates picked out in red, the latter carrying the company's name in full. No. 3 differed in that she was finished in olive green, lined in light green, with the name painted on the centre splasher. Brass nameplates were fitted at a later date, and it is believed

'Ilfracombe Goods' 0−6−0 Hesperus *preparing to leave Kinnerley with the daily Criggion goods, consisting of 18 BQC empties behind a coal-laden PO wagon (J. Crane & Co.?). During the late 'thirties, this train formed part of the S & MR's main line goods working, generally leaving Kinnerley during the late morning for Criggion, and returning to the junction by lunch time, ending the day's services. By this time, 'Colliers' were working most of the services, with the ex-LSWR engine generally being used when traffic was light. 11th September 1938.*   R. K. COPE

that she was painted in blue during her latter years. All three had the buffer beams finished in red, with the number painted on in black, although this was in gold on No. 3's tender. Company identification was carried on the tender sides, Nos. 5 and 6 carrying 'S & MR' in white lettering, and No. 3 carrying 'S & M Rly'. No. 3 lasted in service until

1941, outlasting its sister engines by a number of years. No. 5, the least successful, was taken out of traffic in the late '20s, and was dumped at Kinnerley until being cut up on site in 1932; its boiler, however, was still in good condition, and was put to further use on No. 6. With this boiler, No. 6 lasted a further four years until withdrawal in 1935, whereupon she

Kinnerley shed, with ex-LNWR 'Collier' 0−6−0 No. 8108 and ex-LSWR 'Ilfracombe Goods' 0−6−0 Hesperus, *seen on Bank Holiday Monday, 5th August 1935.*
H. F. WHEELLER

No. 8182, one of the three ex-LNWR 'coal engines' purchased by the S & MR between 1930 and 1932 to replace the ageing ex-LSWR 'Ilfracombe Goods' 0–6–0s. The 'Colliers' remained in LMS livery throughout the 'thirties, although No 8018 was overhauled, repainted in S & MR livery and renumbered '2' during 1939. No. 8182 is seen here shunting one of the ex-MR bogie coaches at Kinnerley goods yard on 4th October 1937. These engines, in company with the sole remaining 'Ilfracombe', worked the Criggion branch goods services during the '30s. R. K. COPE

was stored at Kinnerley dump until being cut up in May 1937. In their latter years, these engines wre mostly used on goods trains, both on the main line and the Criggion branch.

During 1930, it was decided that replacements were needed for those three elderly ex-LSWR engines, and three former main line engines were purchased. This time, LMS (ex-LNWR) machines were chosen, these being 0–6–0s from the Webb Coal Engine or 'Collier' class, which were already vacuum fitted. The first to arrive was LMS No. 8108 in March 1930, followed by 8182 in June 1931, and 8236 in August 1932, built at Crewe in 1874, 1879 and 1881 respectively. On the S & MR, they retained their LMS identity and, together with the sole remaining 'Ilfracombe Goods', immortalized the company in its declining years. The eldest, No. 8108, became the first to need urgent repairs, and disappeared into Kinnerley workshops in 1938, but, due to the company's precarious financial position, the repairs took 18 months to complete. The work, which included a new smokebox, and tyre turning at Crewe Works, was completed in May 1939. She appeared in olive green livery lined out in

Ex-LNWR 'coal engine' 0–6–0 No. 8108 now carrying full S & MR livery, and the allocated number '2'. She is pictured on arrival at Kinnerley with the daily train from Shrewsbury on 30th April 1939, with 4-wheel (ex-MR) Passenger Brake Van No. 1 at the head of the formation. AUTHOR'S COLLECTION

black and white, carrying 'S & M' in yellow on the tender sides, and the number '2' on the cabside. It was intended that the other two would be similarly repainted, but the outbreak of the Second World War and the line's subsequent takeover by the military authorities halted any further repainting work by the company. Instead, all three were turned out by the Army in camouflage green with red lining, and the numbers on the cabsides in white lettering; No. 2 reverted to its former LMS number, 8108. All three were withdrawn in 1945 and sent to the WD dump at Hookagate, where they remained until 1950; having become BR

(Western Region) property during May of that year, they were sent to Swindon Works for cutting up.

All the coaching stock was purchased second-hand from many different sources, and in many different styles, ranging from bogie stock to four-wheelers. Four bogie coaches were purchased from the MR in 1911, together with two 4-wheel passenger full brakes; at the same time, six 4-wheelers, which came from the LSWR (ex-Plymouth, Devonport & South Western Junction Railway) were acquired. A few years later, three NSR 4-wheelers were obtained, whilst in 1912, the famous LCC horse tram was purchased, for use with *Gazelle*. Some time before 1923, the 1848-built LSWR 4-wheel Royal Saloon was procured, followed by an ex-GER 6-wheeler from the Kent & East Sussex Railway during the same decade.

The liveries used on the stock were somewhat varied; the ex-MR vehicles, for example, were initially finished in crimson with gold lettering. By 1923, the standard livery was ultramarine blue with vermilion ends, although by the end of the 20s, this had changed to an overall buff livery.

After the withdrawal of regular passenger services in 1933, most of the stock was stored in the bay platform at Kinnerley. The ex-MR bogie stock was used for the bank holiday specials, which ran for a few more years after the main services had been withdrawn. The daily goods which ran on the Criggion branch after the withdrawal of passenger services made use of the ex-MR 4-wheel full brakes, although it is believed that only one vehicle was in use at any one time.

The goods stock was second-hand too, and came from a multitude of sources. By 1914, the wagon fleet consisted of some 50 vehicles, most of which were out of use by 1930. By this time, the granite from Criggion Quarries was the main source of business which, together with some domestic coal and agricultural traffic, was mostly carried in private owner vehicles and wagons from the 'Big Four' companies. The goods stock livery was grey with white lettering, and because the company did not use goods brake vans, a disc bearing the letters 'LV' was hung on the drawhook of the last vehicle.

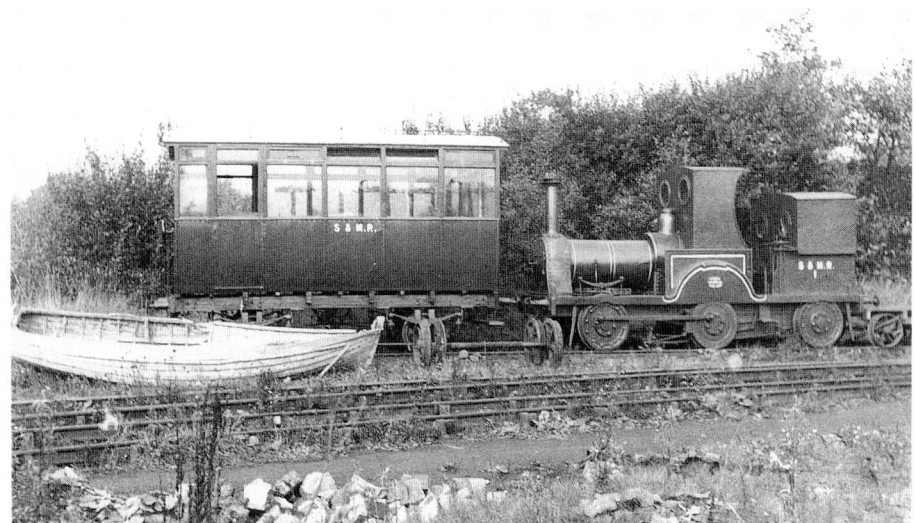

The recently rebuilt Gazelle *in Kinnerley yard on 2nd October 1937, in company with her 'new' coach, which utilised the ex-LCC tramcar chassis with a body from the Selsey Tramway railcar set.*   R. K. COPE

A rake of decaying S & M coaches standing in the former Criggion bay at Kinnerley, on Wednesday, 1st September 1937. These vehicles were latterly used for Bank Holiday and summer excursions, regular passenger services having ceased in 1933. Amongst the coaches are an ex-NSR 4-wheeler, the ex-LSWR Royal Saloon, and a pair of ex-Midland bogie vehicles. Nature is making its presence felt.   R. K. COPE

BRANCH TRAIN SERVICES

Kinnerley station on 27th July 1931, with the Criggion branch empties (made up of Granomac and BQC private owner granite wagons) awaiting departure from the Down platform.
V. R. WEBSTER

Little is known about the train services on the branch prior to the Colonel Stephens era; we can therefore only consider the period from 21st February 1912 (the re-opening for parcels, goods and mineral traffic), passenger traffic commencing in August of that year.

The initial service consisted of two daily return passenger workings, which were entrusted to *Gazelle* and her tramcar coach, together with one return mixed working. The latter utilized any available S & MR locomotive, although the working was usually covered by 0–4–2T *Hecate* (later *Severn*); *Gazelle* covered an additional return passenger working on Wednesday and Saturday mornings. The Sunday service consisted of a solitary return passenger working, which is believed to have been worked by an ordinary locomotive, to enable *Gazelle* to have a washout and any running repairs done; this service proved uneconomical, and was withdrawn during the 1914-18 war.

By the mid 1920s, road transport was beginning to encroach into the available traffic in the area, and by the end of the decade it had developed to such an extent

that economies had to be made over the whole of the S & M system. Needless to say, the Criggion branch service fell within the first wave of cuts, and from September 1928, the passenger service was reduced to Thursdays and Saturdays only. As Melverley viaduct was causing

the company some concern, from October 1932 the service was terminated at Melverley as a safety precaution. However, this arrangement only lasted for just over a year, because all the remaining passenger services on the system were withdrawn from 6th November 1933. After that

A Criggion-bound passenger train passing 'Mushroom Terrace' as it leaves Crew Green station, c.1931, one of the newly acquired ex-LNWR 'coal engines', probably No. 8108, heading a typically 'mixed' formation, with what appears to be the ex-LSWR Royal Saloon, an ex-MR bogie coach, and one of the ex-MR 4-wheel Passenger Brake Vans. A party of Girl Guides occupied the nearest camping hut at the time of the photograph; with black sides and a white roof, it is easy to understand how the structures came by their nickname of 'mushrooms'. The track at this point was liable to flooding when the nearby River Severn became swollen with rain.
MRS. M. CADMAN

SHROPSHIRE AND MONTGOMERYSHIRE RAILWAY

Shrewsbury Station, S. & M.R.

SUPPORT THE LOCAL LINE

Melverley Bridge
(View on River Severn)

Melverley Church (A.D. 1450).

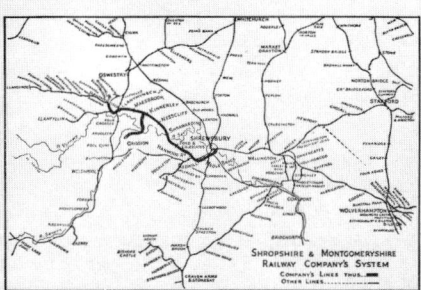

SHROPSHIRE & MONTGOMERYSHIRE
RAILWAY COMPANY'S SYSTEM
COMPANY'S LINES THUS.
OTHER LINES.

Criggion Station and Breidden Hills.

TIME TABLE.

Monday, October 3rd, 1932, and until further notice.

WEEK DAYS ONLY.   WEEK DAYS ONLY.

UP TRAINS.	a.m.	a.m.	a.m.	p.m.	p.m.	p.m.
Llanymynech Jn. S. & M.R. dep.	...	8 10	...	5 0	...	7 35
Maesbrook ... ,,	...	8 15	...	5 5	...	7 40
Wern Las ... ,,		S		S		S
Criggion ... ,,	Saturdays only.		Saturdays only.		Saturdays only.	
Llandrinio Road ... ,,						
Crew Green or ALBERBURY, COEDWAY ,,						
Melverley ... ,,	8 15			3 15		
Chapel Lane ... ,,	S			S		
Kinnerley Junction ... ,,	8 25	8 35 12 30		3 25	5 20	7 50
Edgerley ... ,,		S S			S	
Nesscliff and Pentre ... ,,		8 43 12 40			5 28	
Shrawardine ... ,,		S S			S	
Ford and Crossgates ... ,,		8 56 12 55			5 40	
Shoothill ... ,,		S S			S	
Cruckton ... ,,		S S			S	
Edgebold ... ,,		S S			S	
Hook-a-gate and Redhill ,,		S S			S	
Meole Brace ... ,,		9 15 1 15			6 0	
Shrewsbury West ... ,,		S S			S	
Shrewsbury S. & M.R. arr.		9 30 1 30			6 10	

DOWN TRAINS.	a.m.	a.m.	a.m.	p.m. Sats. only.	p m.	p.m.	p.m.
Shrewsbury, S. & M.R. dep.		...	10 15	1 45	...	...	6 20
Shrewsbury West ... ,,			S	S		...	S
Meole Brace ... ,,			10 30	2 0		...	6 30
Hook-a-gate and Redhill ,,			S	S			S
Edgebold ... ,,			S	S			S
Cruckton ... ,,			S	S			S
Shoot Hill ... ,,			S	S			S
Ford and Crossgates ,,			10 45	2 20			6 45
Shrawardine ... ,,	Saturdays only.		S	S		Saturdays only.	S
Nesscliff and Pentre ,,			11 0	2 35			7 0
Edgerley ... ,,			S	S			S
Kinnerley Junction ... ,,	8 07	3 0 11 10		2 45	3 04	3 0 7 10	
Chapel Lane ... ,,		S		S		S	
Melverley ... ,,	8 10			3 10			
Crew Green for ALBERBURY, COEDWAY ,,							
Llandrinio Road ... ,,							
Criggion ... ,,							
Wern Las ... ,,		S				S	S
Maesbrook ... ,,		7 40				4 40 7 20	
Llanymynech Jn.S.&M.R. arr.		7 45				4 45 7 25	

Note S.—Stops by signal to pick up and set down passengers on notice being given at Station or to Guard on joining Train.

A reasonable amount of Market produce can be carried Free on all trains and will be conveyed Free from the Abbey Station to the Market Hall, Shrewsbury.

The times shewn on the Time Table are the times before which the respective Trains will not start from the various Stations.

Special Excursion Fares are in operation between all stations.

CHEAP MARKET TICKETS issued from all stations TO SHREWSBURY DAILY; Cheap Market Tickets issued from all stations to Welshpool, on Mondays, to Oswestry on Wednesdays and Saturdays and to Llanfyllin, on Thursdays. (See handbills.)

BOATING AND FISHING on the Rivers Severn and Vyrnwy. Pleasure boats obtainable at Melverley Bridge, Crew Green Station.

SEASON TICKETS issued between any Stations at Reduced Rates.

The Company have 5 CAMPING HUTS at Crew Green, Rental 7/- per week.

SPECIAL TRIPS arranged for Parties, at Reduced Rates.

THROUGH RATES for Parcels and Goods traffic can be arranged with all Stations in British Isles.

CARTAGE facilities are available for all classes of Traffic to and from each Station.

JAMES RAMSAY,
Managing Director.

Shrewsbury,
September, 1932.

LIVESEY LTD., PRINTERS, SHREWSBURY.

date, the only passenger trips seen on the line were the summer excursions (although they ceased in 1937) and specials.

The final passenger timetable was introduced from 6th February 1933, and consisted of a 7.30 a.m. Kinnerley to Llanymynech, with an 8.10 a.m. return working which continued to Shrewsbury, arriving at 9.30 a.m.; the train departed at 10.15 a.m. to Kinnerley, after which the stock was shunted into the sidings at Kinnerley depot. On Saturdays, there was an additional morning return trip from Kinnerley to Melverley. In the afternoon, there was a 2.30 p.m. working from Kinnerley to Shrewsbury, which returned at 3.45 p.m. and ran through to Melverley, arriving at 5.00 p.m. The train was then propelled back to Kinnerley, arriving at 5.15 p.m., after which it resumed its journey to Llanymynech; the return trip to Kinnerley completed the passenger workings. The Saturday services were the most favoured by the 'locals', although only one ticket was issued from Llanymynech to Criggion during the 1927 to 1931 period! During the branch's final months, with services terminating at Melverley, a single coach sufficed, which, because there was no loop at Melverley, was propelled in one direction.

The only other working was the Monday to Friday daily freight train, which mostly consisted of the BQC stone traffic with the occasional load of coal and general merchandise for one of the intermediate stations; this working remained more or less the same until closure in 1959. To give some idea of the traffic density during the 1935 to 1948 period, the goods statistics for 1947 were:

Despatched	340 tons Goods
	30 tons Coal
	20,761 tons Minerals
Received	20 tons Goods
	241 tons Coal
	30 tons Minerals

BQC stone tonnages from Criggion during this twelve month period consisted of 846 loaded wagons.

The branch was always worked on the 'one engine in steam' principle although, in the pre-Colonel Stephens era, the wayside stations were signalled. When the line was downgraded to light railway status, these, together with the level crossing gates, were removed, and a general speed limit of 25 mph (reduced to 10 mph on curves of less than 9 chains radius, or within 300 yards of unprotected level crossings) was imposed.

As previously mentioned, the branch was originally laid using bullhead rails and chairs. Just prior to 1939, portions were relaid with flat-bottom rails on 'new' (second-hand) sleepers, further sections being similarly treated during the 1940s.

Gradients were fairly easy, the line rising gently in the Criggion direction, and also on both approaches to Melverley viaduct. The mineral trains normally consisted of between 5 and 10 loaded wagons, with about 15 or so when returning empty, and obviously experienced very few difficulties. By the late 1930s, it was this traffic that kept the whole of the

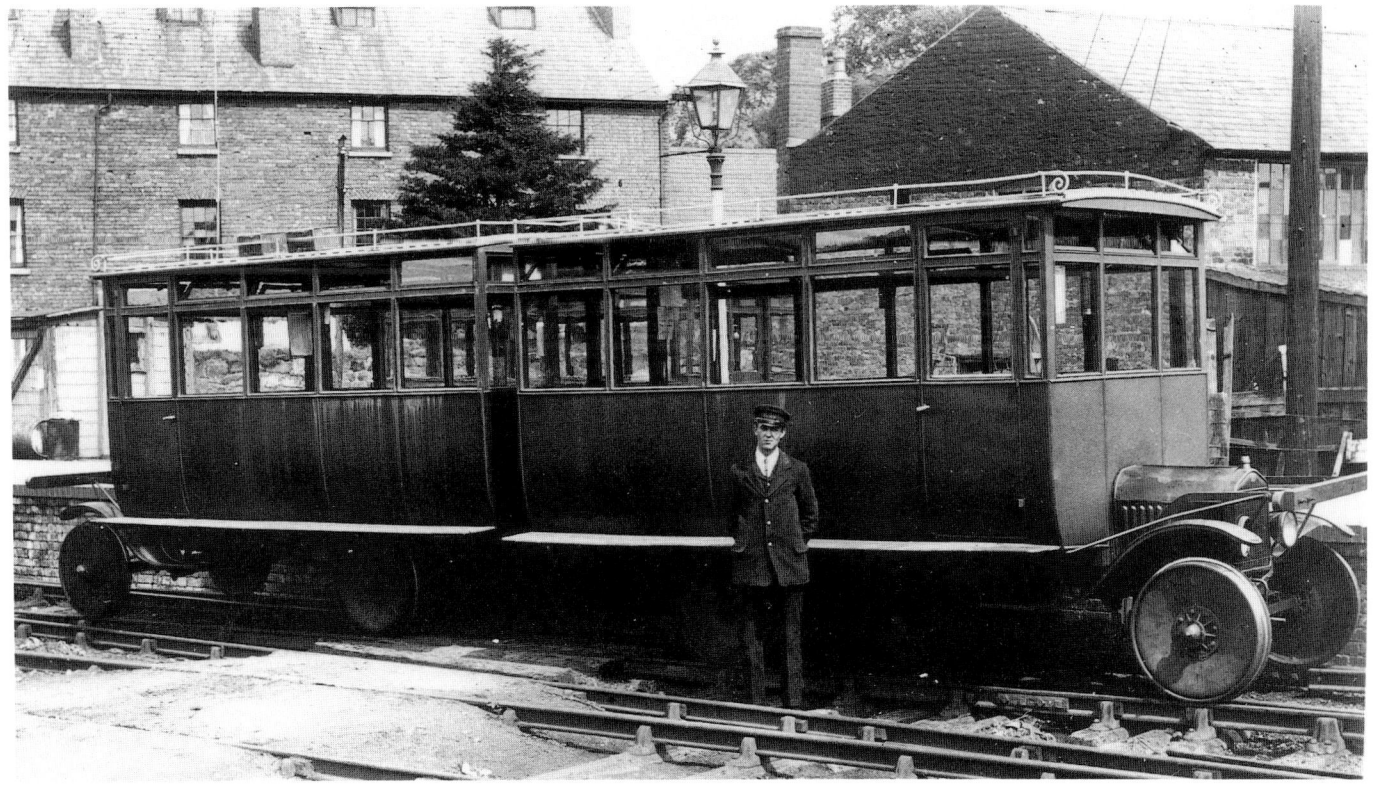

During its final years of operation, the Criggion branch passenger service was worked by the Ford railcar set, shown here at Shrewsbury Abbey station c.1928. Built and delivered in a pleasing shade of blue in 1923, this was one of two railcar sets on the S & MR, the other being constructed by Wolseley-Siddeley. Both sets proved unpopular, the Wolseley more so; this was withdrawn in 1929, whilst the Ford soldiered on until about 1936, spending much of the 1928-30 period on the Criggion branch services. Upon withdrawal, both sets were put out to grass at Kinnerley; the Wolseley was scrapped in 1935, whilst the Ford survived until 1941. Each set had engines in both vehicles, the unit to the rear (according to the direction of travel) being disengaged. The Ford set was provided with extra vehicles, which could be added depending upon traffic requirements. One of these was a trailer coach, built by Edmunds of Thetford, whilst the other was a single unit goods vehicle, which could also operate as part of the set.
LENS OF SUTTON

A view of Shrewsbury (Abbey) station, looking towards the buffer stops on 5th July 1936.
S. W. BAKER

S & MR going, and it is interesting to look at the outgoing stone tonnages from Ceiriog Quarry, Criggion, during this period:

Date	Total Tonnage	Via Main Line Coys.	To S & MR Stations
1935	40,186	34,990	5,196
1936	22,485	18,747	3,738
1937	18.931	16,143	2,788
1938	17,116	13,469	3,467
1939	15,000 approx.	15,000 approx.	Nil*

* In 1939, rail transport was considered to be uneconomical for transportation of stone over short distances.

The stone carried was usually broken, or in chippings, but occasionally consignments of large pieces were conveyed, for use in foundation or sea defence work.

During 1940-41, when Melverley viaduct was temporarily out of use, all rail traffic was concentrated at Four Crosses station, GWR. It is interesting to note that when the newly formed BQC secured a contract to supply 200,000 tons of road stone for the East Lancashire road scheme in 1929 (when there were exceptionally high tonnages carried over the S & MR from Criggion), the deliveries continued for a number of years afterwards. The peak was reached in 1931, when over 140,000 tons were carried, and the S & MR made a record profit of £1,660.

Incoming traffic consisted mainly of materials associated with agriculture:

Looking down the branch from Shrewsbury (Abbey) station on 5th August 1935.
H. F. WHEELLER

manures, fertilisers, cattle cake, feedstuffs, meal, cement, bricks and coal, all of which traffic had become quite light by the late 1930s. Private owner wagons were frequently seen on the branch; in particular, Hanwood wagons supplied 'hand coal', whilst Littleton vehicles conveyed 'cobbles'.

Other significant outgoing traffic during the period consisted of some general goods and agricultural produce. During the Great War (and up to 1919), large rounds of timber from the Breidden Hills, mainly oak and larch, were loaded at Criggion by a contractor, Messrs. Cadman & Co. of Birmingham and Stoke. A cattle pen was provided at Llandrinio Road station to handle the small consignments of livestock, although this traffic had largely ceased by the 'thirties.